LOVE'S fingerprints

By Bernard Horn

Our Daily Words
Facing the Fires: Conversations with A. B. Yehoshua

LOVE'S
fingerprints

BERNARD
HORN
POEMS

CIRCLING RIVERS
RICHMOND, VIRGINIA

Copyright © 2020 Bernard Horn

All rights reserved. No part of this book may be reproduced in any form, including electronic, without permission in writing from the author.

CIRCLING RIVERS
PO Box 8291
Richmond, VA 23226

www.CirclingRivers.com

ISBN: 978-1-939530-09-7 | paper
Library of Congress Control Number: 2020938880

ISBN: 978-1-939530-13-4 | hardcover
Library of Congress Control Number: 2020938957

Cover art:
Linda Klein, Messy Fingerprints, drawing
Author photograph by Leslie Starobin
    copyright © 2019 | www.starobinartworks.com

Visit CirclingRivers.com to subscribe to news of our authors and books, including book giveaways. We never share or sell our list.

For Linda,
and
for Lyla, Louis, and Roni

                It is late
but an odor
        as from our wedding
                has revived for me
and begun again to penetrate
        into all crevices
                of my world.

from "Asphodel, That Greeny Flower," by William Carlos Williams

Contents

Dedication | 5
Self-Portrait with Music | 13

I. Hear!

Sunday in the Park | 17
The Work of Our Hands | 18
The Porch | 20
The Black Corduroy Blazer | 22
To My Brother | 24
Portrait of My Mother Knitting | 26
My Father, the Swimmer | 28
Baseball | 44
Wind Hair | 46
Opera | 48
The Merit of Ancestors | 50

II. Dreams of a Black Panther

Valentine 2014 | 61
Cinderella | 62
Basketball | 63
At Capo Vaticano | 64
My Daughter | 67
Asphaltene | 68
Forty-Five Years Ago | 69
The Widower | 70
Recognitions | 71
The Dinner | 72
At the Movies | 73
After the Rehearsal | 74
Sappho's Blues: Four Songs | 76
"Easy Come" | 81
In Provincetown | 82
Aubade: Wonderland | 84
Dreams of a Black Panther | 86

III. Red Red

Any Misery in the Sound of the Wind | 92
The Snorkelers | 93
Betrayal | 94
On Ahad Ha'am Street | 95
Late December Nightfall | 97
Laughable | 99
Raccoon | 100
Ankle | 102
Above Leuk | 103
What I Knew | 104
Sycamores | 106
Red Red | 107

IV. The Ideal World

The Silence | 110
Mind, Feel | 112
Strange Love | 113
Schubert | 115
Death, Rothko Said | 116
Hope. Heartbreak. | 117
He Rises: A Vision, January 2, 2020 | 120
Five Consolations | 122
The Ideal World | 123
To My Wife | 124
Earthsea | 125
Still, Small | 127
The City | 128
Home | 129

Notes | 131
Acknowledgments | 133

LOVE'S fingerprints

Self-Portrait with Music

Nothing changes, said the husband,
everything changes, said the wife,
in my favorite story. As for me, I like the going back and
forth between deep and narrow Hebrew
and wide flat American and losing myself
in the translation. I take SPACE said my teacher
to be the central fact to man born in America.
In Israel I love the intimacy, the long
eyes meeting eyes in Mediterranean cafes,
and the loneliness. If such eyes had turned toward
the brutes of our time when they were
desperate ten-year-olds, would they vanish
like smoke? As for despair,
I remember the consolation of staring for hours
at Robin's watercolor above the mantle, a landscape
he'd painted from memory at eighty,
while the chords of Schubert's two-cello quintet
eroded my pain, the way, just the other day,
"Spanish Harlem" sung a cappella on our friend's CD
dissolved the car anguish
of our baby granddaughter,
during a four-hour trip—how we gratefully
replayed the song dozens of times.
I take TIME to be the central fact
to anyone born in Jerusalem. I've taken on
the reciting of kaddish for an Israeli friend,
since November. Her symphony is not unfinished—it's just
that, in another life, the melody in the Andante
would go on, repeating itself forever. I love
to watch my own wife in passionate colloquy,
far enough away that her sentences are cadences.
I am not my father's son. I am

my father's son. My brother always
calls me before I call him
with something on his mind. In Sinai I see myself
snorkeling off Sharm el-Sheikh, floating,
out of time, as luminous fish of many colors
swim from my dreams into this green transparency,
the way the birds displaced from the rift valley,
their resting place for millennia, returned immediately
when the valley was reflooded, a scatter of pelicans
and the eighty thousand cranes that made my spirits soar
last October. I wish our nation could heal as the earth does,
given half a chance…and my grandchildren . . .
how they may see to it.
I'd like finally to learn the piano. I wish
I could be sure of my courage. I hope
I get to whisper to my breath to go.

I. Hear!

Sunday in the Park

Today I'm thinking about a summer Sunday afternoon
in van Cortland, my father showing off with a soccer ball
to his European immigrant buddies–obviously,
he really was a star as a teen in Poland–though he'd
never dispute his pals' grand recollections over gin rummy
Saturday nights–not one peep from his lips!–
while I played second base in a pickup softball game
and missed an easy pop-up and a grounder too
because I kept throwing glances his way.
You are dead thirty years.
That day in the park was nearly sixty years
ago, I was twelve, and you were too
strong and near to be a symbol
of anything. Who will remember you
easily heading the ball between makeshift goal markers
past two defenders and a goalie, when I die,
too? Who will remember I'd caught your eye
in the park that day and realized you'd been watching
me, too, the two of us in clandestine complicity,
as, in the old tales, a princess peeks out
from behind a trellis and a slightly pulled back curtain
at the moment when her forbidden lover
passes by below on the street each day
and sneaks a glance up at her window?

The Work of Our Hands

Whenever I turn up the heat and the force
of the shower to rinse shampoo
from my hair, I think of my mother
when I was three or four at bath's end,
holding one hand over the tap
to create a fountain of spray, as the other sifts
the soap from my hair and keeps my head
from banging against the heavy faucet of the deep
clawfoot tub. She was almost forty. At ten,
she witnessed her father's murder in his living room
in the Ukraine, at twenty, she brought
her aging, half-unwilling mother
across Europe, the Atlantic, and half of Canada,
from Uman to Winnipeg, and at thirty-three,
she left her own beloved extended family there
and led her husband and three-year-old son
to New York–1700 miles by rail–to escape a sister-in-law
bent on dismantling her marriage. Outside,
this gray day in fine rain
I worked the garden plot
I'd spent hours in yesterday, the muddy soil
still infested with the white, worm-like
roots of the thick ground cover.
Bishop's Weed. On my hands and knees,
I bear my cultivator down and yank it upwards
with a twist, my mud-sodden work gloves
slipping a bit as whole chunks
tear free–soil, dark root tendrils,
and those undulating white shoots entangled
in the wide tines, along with a rising earthy
smell, the rich whiff of an abandoned cellar,
the chill, as I notice I've run my muddy gloved hand

through my dripping eyebrows upward,
along my forehead and my hair,
and, Mother, my eyes are blurred and I'm dreaming
of a thick hot spray of cleansing water from the tap:
your fierce independence
absorbed on that occasion
in the work of deft attentive hands.

The Porch

After Philip Levine

The splintery wooden stairs leading up to the large porch
of the sprawling Victorian rooming house is mottled
black and bright from the wrought iron light fixture
suspended over the center of the octagonal poker table,
and the banter of the six players around the table
in their wicker chairs reaches you
at the bottom of the stairs, so you pause
there. You're filled with the joy that comes to a great athlete
when his body has astonished him again, a few droplets
of salt water glinting from your skin. You'd left your narrow
high-ceilinged housewares store on Avenue D,
stopped in your rented room, where I waited for you,
exchanged short-sleeved shirt and slacks
and leather shoes for sandals, towel, and bathing suit,
and headed to the ocean, where you swam
through and beyond the breakers,
far beyond the rotted jetties, as the sun set
and you vanished in the distance and the darkness
of a moonless Saturday night in July, alone
except for the eight-year-old boy staring out at the sea
from the galvanized boardwalk railing,
as he did every week. You're ravenous now
at the foot of the stairs and you know
your wife has ladled out
blistering hot chicken soup with kreplach
into the green glass summer soup bowl
on the faded Formica table, and the six others
you play with every week will deal you in
whenever you come down
to the nickel-and-dime poker game, no small stakes

for the seven of you in the 1950s,
shopkeepers, garment workers,
butchers and grocers, who were taking one
or two days off each week from the ten-hour
workdays of summer in the city. Harry Horn,
let me enter your story as you stand
motionless in the speckled light
at the bottom of the stairs breathing
the rich salty air. Don't go up yet. Let your
mind take you back to the powerful strokes
that pulled you far into the Atlantic,
fearless over very deep water,
or, entirely at your ease,
floating on your back out there, your chest glowing
faintly in the moonlight as your breath reaches in
and out, deeply, and your eyes
open wide to the vast canopy
of glittering and exploding stars.

The Black Corduroy Blazer

There's something amusing, or dreamy,
about how methodically I linger
over every jacket in one
packed rack at the designer's outlet,
doggedly shopping, trying on the handful
among them neither extra-long,
nor massive, nor skimpy, many, despite their high-
toned designer labels, so shoddily sewn
and assembled somewhere that seams are
loosening, buttons barely hang on, threads
dangle, though they haven't even been worn,
but only tried on a few times
at most. I pry one coat
from the rack, finger
the fabric, tug the seams, examine
the lining, the buttons and buttonholes:
a black wide wale corduroy blazer,
with hand-braided dark brown leather buttons.

My mother, a math prodigy
who never went to college, took on seamstress work
to help the family make ends meet. "Save up,"
she'd say. "Buy one good suit, one good
pair of pants, a couple of fine double-stitched
shirts, top-of-the-line ties, fabrics of
quality (she'd run her thumb firmly along the pads
of her other fingers): wools, silks, heavy-weight
cottons, that feel good on your skin and look
good in the mirror." The mayhem she had known
taught her a
simple calculation: "Don't skimp
on the tailoring," she'd say.

"You'll save money in the long run.
Buy clothes to last, to live with."

Relined ten years back,
the jacket's still there in my closet
thirty years later, lush.

To My Brother

After his second heart attack we would find our father
    lying there on his back
        suspended in the intricate nest
of valves, needles, wires, and tubes
    in uneasy sleep,
        the fingers of both
hands clenched
    to white knuckles
        around the rails of his hospital bed.
We would try
    to pry his fingers
        free, thinking
to comfort.
    To no avail. His grip
        was just too strong. When he came to,
he did an almost comic double-take,
    at me, standing
        at the foot of his bed
and said
    between gasps for breath
        that he had
felt a massive weight
    on the middle of his chest,
        pressing him downward
toward the great black depths below him.
    "I almost gave up," he said,
        then he saw
our four arms reaching down to him
    over the lip of the abyss.
        "I grabbed tight hold of your hands,"
he said more than forty years ago,
    "and pulled myself out

  by desire…
for the next
  few years
    of your lives."

Portrait of My Mother Knitting

This is not my mother, I think,
this portrait of Madame Boissière,
whom Caillebotte painted in black
a hundred thirty years ago, intent, lips pursed,
bent over her knitting in an ornate,
high-backed wooden chair
in the shallow space she shares
with a tall buffet, a swirl of floral color
only in the flock on the walls, and two white skeins of yarn
like clouds, in baskets on the empty dining room table.

Yes, she's knitting, too, but she's alone
while my mother would beat an under-rhythm
for all of us on her needles
as we watched TV or chatted
in the living room or returned
to the beach blanket for tuna on rye,
ripe tomatoes and hard-boiled eggs
to salt and bite into,
after splashing around in the Atlantic
till our lips were blue,

she, easy and upright
in her folding beach chair
or her cozy armchair in the living room–

"Clickclick. Clickclick," my father would say,
good-naturedly as he knitted the air with his hands,
drawing the most demure of smiles
to her lips and eyes–
a rare instance of teasing banter
between my parents–

both long gone now.

Her knitting was one of the last things
to leave her, and this autumn
my wife has taken to wrapping herself in
the present my mother knitted
for my sixteenth birthday: a heavy
two-toned gray sweater with a
soaring green-headed pheasant
red and black wings outspread
on the back and silhouettes of a hunter
and a dog on the front
it still keeps the fall chill off our bones.

My Father, the Swimmer

August 1977 / August 1952

DID WE SPEAK TO EACH other during the short walk from the rented room or bungalow to the beach, my hand lost in yours, my legs scurrying to keep up? What does stay in my mind is sitting on the boardwalk railing at Rockaway Beach, the zinc coating of the pipe always damp in the salty ocean air and slightly rough. I'm eight or nine. It's easy to conjure the two of us still outside in the eight o'clock light of a hot August evening. You'd picked me after a ten-hour day in your narrow housewares and toy store on Avenue D; whenever I entered the store as a kid, it was like entering the bottom of a chasm, the shelves in the walls nooks and crannies containing anything anyone could imagine, somewhere between the floor and the high, high ceiling. I remember how you used to leap upwards, precariously balanced at the edges of the shelves to retrieve some object, a Monopoly game or a boxed toaster, from the uppermost shelf–you'd maneuver the box free with your fingertips or a ruler and then you'd leap down, and as you landed, lightly, the box would come to rest right-side-up in your arms.

It's the early fifties. The low income projects, named for turn-of-the-twentieth-century social reformers and muckrakers–Jacob Riis, Lilian Wald–that fill the one block from the H & D Housewares Company to the East River, have not yet become less habitable than the decayed tenements above and alongside the store. It's years before the junkies and young thugs become so cocky and unpredictable that you—always on good terms with an earlier generation of thieves and hustlers (though you never handled their stolen goods)—even you began to close early, no longer able to rely on your good name and the heavy stick–was it an ax handle?– you kept below the cash register. At the time you had no way of knowing you had already embarked on the grinding march towards your unwilling sale of that store in 1963, fifteen years after you'd scraped together enough money and experience to open your own business with Mr. Davidson, who had less experience and more money, in a partnership sealed by a handshake after only two conversations.

I remember your words. "That Davidson. Never sick a day in his life. And when his stomach starts acting up, he makes jokes: *Your ulcer is lonely,* he liked to say, *so my belly decided to keep it company.* He used to take a shot of whiskey, first one, then two, even three times a day." He always told you how good he felt afterwards, *how he was burning the sickness away.*

"Poor Davidson!" you'd say before launching into a pitch-perfect evocation of your friend and partner. *"Harry,* he'd say, *Harry, you know why you're sick all the time? It's on account of you're always rushing off to doctors. It's been a good ten years since I seen one, and that was the time I cut my arm on that pane of glass. Fourteen stitches, and I was back to work the next day."*

You always smiled and shook your head at the number, fourteen, as you are doing right now. And when Davidson finally gave in to you and Mother and his wife Sylvia, and went to the doctor, his insides were so riddled with cancer he was gone in six weeks. I've always associated Davidson's death with Uncle Yossel's comment, after he, another supremely healthy man, also got nailed by cancer. "S'hot mir g'catched." *It caught me.*

It took more than twenty years, but you got caught, too. A stroke. Here we sit, you in your wheel chair, the soul of your language shattered to atoms, I talking and thinking to you about the past, and I have no certainty my words are getting through any better than my thoughts, not knowing if that smile and nod at "fourteen stitches" merely mirrored my gesture or the tone of my voice.

And as I sink into this Naugahyde hospital chair here in Manhattan, it's easy for me to feel the dampness and roughness of those zinc-painted beach railings squeeze through my shorts and chill my darkly tanned thighs as I adjust my legs around the rail and I look down and I'm wearing yellow shorts, polished brown shoes, and white socks sliding down into them. It's 1952, August, night.

I look up. You are getting smaller, briskly walking toward the breakers in a gray boxer bathing suit, a yellow towel around your shoulders, your very white skin glowing in the moonlight. You bend, unbuckle your sandals, fold the towel neatly on top of them, and carefully top the heap with your glasses. The sand has lost its brown tincture, the Atlantic Ocean is black, and the foam from the breaking waves glints more brightly than your skin. Now the sound reaches me across the years and I watch you enter the water, walk out till the bottom of your bathing suit gets wet, and you take a double handful of water and slosh it against your face. I don't know if I saw you clearly that time from the boardwalk, or if I've seen you enter the water so many times that way my mind fills in the details: the slight white splash as you dive in, your hands and forearms as they cut through the water. You swim out, far out, way over your head. As I lose sight of you, I start playing my nightly game of guessing which sudden splash of white in the distance is you, and it always scares me a little as I try to trace your path, deeper and further, and my imagination always betrays me—I'm always surprised by your location when on moonlit nights I catch clear sight of you emerging from the water. Other nights, it's so dark by then, I'm still looking out at the Atlantic when I hear you walking through the sand, suddenly just a few strides from the wooden stairs that rise from the beach to the boardwalk. You're full of joy and drops of water.

"There's nothing like it. Nothing in the whole world," you say, only partly to me.

It was during the first week after you were stricken that you began to play with the finger of your right hand. I was still jet-lagged from my twelve-hour flight from Kennedy to Ben Gurion and twenty-four hours of wakefulness. You lifted first the small finger, then the ring finger, then the middle finger, one by one, the hand hanging palm downward, hooklike in its sling, and you watched with what seemed like detached curiosity, as each finger in its turn, then your hand, sprang back downward to its lifeless dangling. You continued for about fifteen minutes, sometimes plucking one finger three or four times, sometimes holding the hand or finger still for a few seconds before letting it drop.

Then you looked up at me and you sagged.

It was that afternoon you cooperated for the first time with the physical therapist. Those brief bursts of bitterly sarcastic laughter you had fired at Mother and me vanished for good, along with your attempts to tear the covers from your bed, the IV tube from your arm, the feeding tube from your nose, and the condom catheter from your penis and your terrible cries of "ber BELL! ber BELL! ber BELL!" which I heard as "I'm well! I'm well! I'm well!—why am I tied up like this?"

Don't get me wrong. I'm not saying you have become sanguine about your condition. You still, on occasion, shake your fist at me or clench my forearm in your good left hand in anger or despair and far too often weep small tears, bitter and sad puzzlement in your eyes.

Summer 1948

SUNDAYS AT THE BEACH, I'M four, and you are wrapped in towels, a plaid cotton bathrobe, and a white canvas hat, a few patches of your skin showing, on a green shaded beach chair with white fringes. My legs and arms are chubby and chocolate brown from long days in the sun. Mother sits on her beach chair, reads, feeds all of us, talks to her friends, knits, and periodically "takes a dip" with "the girls." These dips consist of going into the water, hunkering down a little, knees bent, back to the waves, and letting the splash and spray of the ocean slide and splatter up her back to her shoulders. She adored the ocean breezes, the salt air, the salt water, but I don't recall ever seeing her face in the water. She never swam, as she never danced.

As for you, I've never seen anyone swim as you did. I love how you swam, and, for years, before anyone taught me the ins and outs of the crawl, I tried in my bungling way to teach myself your stroke. Your head and the top of your shoulders always stay above the water. Your white arms come out, then quickly slice into the water, leaving barely a ripple. It looks so neat and effortless I wouldn't know the power of your stroke if I weren't riding on your back, my hands holding your collar bones, or holding on to your neck for dear life as you pull us toward the deep water. Sometimes it is the pause and slide, pause and slide of the breaststroke which I know you could do forever, or you cradle me in front of you as you side-stroke along, or your arms envelop me, making my own private little pool in the Atlantic.

That was the center of all those Sundays: you taking me "out for a swim." Out there, alone with you in the Atlantic Ocean, I feel no more than a trace, a tremor, of the fear I later felt when swimming at the top of very deep water—no, time and time again, I'm so caught up, so mastered by your power and the tides, I don't notice until we are far out, way past the end of the rotting wooden jetties, that we are alone out there, that the umbrellas on the shore are tiny splotches of color, and the swimmers between us and the beach shine in the distance like tarnished dimes.

July 1977

I ALSO REMEMBER OUR HOPE during those first weeks, and the weight of small gestures. The good left hand touching the right a week after the stroke, the good arm lifting the right arm and massaging it three days later. The *stand* syllable of *understand* spoken clearly. I remember your attention and focus. These were the days of small angers, small gestures, your sorrow gentle, resigned, peaceful. I remember thinking of a spread in the old *Life* magazine on the latest procedures in medicine: page after red glistening page–the blood, the paper-pages I stared at in fascination. One series of images remains engraved in my mind. A clawlike, shiny right hand with one long cut and four crosscuts on the knuckles; from the wound oozes white calcified muck. In the next photograph, a scalpel scrapes the stuff away. The last shows a newly stitched hand, an image of the hand of Frankenstein's creature. I imagine your stroke as that white poison and I imagine scraping the speech sections of your cerebrum clear of the muck, and then you would speak.

Three and a half weeks after the stroke, you sat in your wheel chair with a crumpled napkin in your left hand. Three times, straining to keep my voice flat, I said, "Throw it to me." You nodded, yes, definitely, each time. You did not toss the napkin. Your eyes caught mine and then narrowed as you searched my face, and tears appeared in their corners.

Summer 1968

THERE WAS YOUR VISIT TO my cottage in Connecticut, at the lake while I was in grad school. I had rented a barely winterized three-room shack at $100 a month; during the summers these shacks are bungalows that go for $300 a week, but my absentee landlord who lived way up in Maine was happy with my sure $1200 a year.

It was late on a summer afternoon. You'd just arrived. You immediately throw on a bathing suit and head down to the lake. I'm five minutes behind you.

I run down the hill to the beach, kick off my sandals, put down my towel and glasses near yours, and run onto the dirty sand. There was no one else to be seen.

You aren't a head and arms in motion way out from the shore. No, you stand erect in the water up to your thighs, the bottom of your bathing suit wet, hands at your sides, still. I stop a couple of yards to your left. Tears pour from your eyes the way a child cries, and you make no effort to conceal them or wipe them away. "What is it, Dad?" You don't speak, and I realize both of us had forgotten about your heart attacks, the massive one two winters before and the second one the following fall.

That was the third time I saw you cry.

July 1977

ABOUT A MONTH AFTER THE stroke, you wrote a note to Mother on which I'm sure I could decipher angry and sorry, though your handwriting deteriorated after the first couple of letters. The next day you wrote—I think, only the *wh* was clear—*Why* and *What*. The next day your writing was indecipherable, but when I wrote *Why*, you said it clearly. The next day was a day of rage and resistance, particularly directed at Mother, but in the midst of it all, when you were in the toilet and wanted out, you yelled her name distinctly, and later when you spotted me at the other end of the building where I'd parked myself, unobserved I thought, to take in your interaction with the physical therapist, you called my name.

As I approached you, I fell into a recollection of my first few trips to school, riding two city buses in Brooklyn from Williamsburg to Crown Heights when I was seven and beginning third grade. How you would follow me at a distance, get on the bus the last moment, and travel with me all the way to school, making believe you were unobserved! How I never acknowledged your presence and I loved you for doing exactly what you did! That night at the hospital, after I walked over to you, I pressed your hands silently together, to exercise your right hand with your left, and you shouted, "Shut up!" and both of us cracked up.

Winter 1956

THE DARKNESS AT 4:30 OR so in the afternoon in my memory makes me certain it is December. I'm twelve, walking home from school down St. Nicholas Avenue with four other kids–you know them all–Harvey Strauss, Larry Oppenheimer, and the two biggest boys in the seventh grade, Donny Goldman and Kenny Weinberg. We are the last to leave school–I don't know whether we were just fooling around or whether one or two of us had been kept late for some transgression. Come to think of it, I bet Donny had been nailed for talking back or out of turn. He took me under his wing when I arrived as the new boy in the class a few weeks after school had started. He let me share his cubbyhole. We're best friends.

The wide street is empty. Scraps of paper spin in the wind against the gray sky. It amazes me how clearly I can see it all. As we walk by the big paint store, all of us carrying the stuffed leather school bags which always made me feel a little silly, we are playing saloojee, which my daughters many years later in Massachusetts, will call "Keep away," with Harvey's brown leather hat with attached ear muffs. "C'mon Straussie,

Straussie, Straussie," Donnie is bugging him. The next thing I know three red-faced Irish kids about our age, bigger than me, smaller than Donny and Kenny, collide into our game. On purpose.

To this day, I can't put my finger on what tipped me off. Maybe the rising pitch in the biggest one's voice when he says, "You look like you're having a good time." Maybe they seem too calm as all eight of us come to a stop in the middle of the empty sidewalk. There is nobody else around. The only sound is Harvey mumbling as he scrambles to get his hat back on. He jams it on so fast it is a lopsided but no one laughs. My friends look all over the place in silence. Try as I do, I can't catch anyone's eye.

My mind flashes to Raymond Duffy picking a fight with me after Hebrew School, back in Brooklyn. "Take your Jew cap off," he'd said. "I don't wanna insult your religion," before he walloped me in the mouth.

I am sure we are in for a fight.

The biggest kid grins. "We wanna play too. But you know the rules. We're pros. You have to pay us to play with you."

I let my schoolbag go. It thuds against the ground. It's five of us against three of them, and I'd seen Donny pick two eighth graders up and squeeze them around their waists until they gave up.

"Look," the biggest one says, "it'll only cost you ten cents apiece—*oooph!*"

I charge and my head smashes into the middle of his chest. My arms are punching and I hear a loud grunt. Then somebody punches me hard in the back, and somebody else kicks the side of my right calf. I fall forward, hit the sidewalk and slide, scraping my forehead. I twist my head and see the one I smashed into sitting in front of me gasping, His two friends lean over me.

My four friends run like hell down the street, their schoolbags swinging and banging against their legs, Harvey shoving his hat back on his head akimbo every two or three strides. I try to yell. "Donny! Kenny!" come out as gasps. A drop of blood splats on the sidewalk. I touch my forehead. It feels like it's on fire, and there is blood on my hand. Screaming and yelling, I try to get up. But they are on me, twisting my left arm behind my back, punching, kicking. Someone gets his fist in my hair and pulls my head back. The leader slaps me as hard as he can across the face. His friends hold my face against the sidewalk while he goes through my pockets, grunting, "You lousy little kike, you lousy little kike," as I twist and scream.

Then they are gone. I get to my feet and stand there, panting roughly. My books, pencils, pens, hat, and schoolbag are scattered for half a block. There are people in the street again, stepping over and around the debris of the battle. Where did they all come from all of a sudden, I wonder. They steer clear, none of them breaking stride, no one so much as brushing against me. I begin to gather in my damaged goods. I don't know whether I told you this then or not, but I remember noticing most of the English books were scarred in one way or another, the bindings or pages torn or crumpled, but they'd left the Hebrew books alone—the *chumash*, the history book, even the grammar book— as if they feared some wicked Jew magic in the ancient letters.

By the time I get home, I had cooked up a detailed story for Mother. I'm pretty sure it was something about crashing into Donny (I am absolutely sure I stuck him in my lie) during a punchball game right after school. I know she suspects something is fishy, and I spend the next couple of hours listening in dread from my room every time she makes a move in the kitchen, every time the phone rings in the living room, every time she even passes anywhere near the phone, sure she would call Mrs. Goldman or Mrs. Weinberg or one of them would call and the truth would come out.

When she gets ready to leave for her mah jongg game at 7:30, I am so relieved I barely distinguish her words as she, once again, gives me the weekly instructions that made dinner with you something of a chore. Turn on a small flame under the soup and under the pot roast at 8:00. Make sure you sit with your father and keep him company. You know how he likes to eat the boiling hot soup too fast.

By the time I hear your key in the lock, I had dialed Donny's number four times, twice hanging up after a couple of rings, once hanging up when I heard Mrs. Goldman's voice (Do you remember her? Did you ever meet her? She was the tallest, the youngest, the most beautiful of all of the mothers, she was Israeli, with long black hair in a braid, and a slight accent so different from the European accents of your friends.) The fourth time I call I hang up on Donny himself.

Though sometimes I would shout a hello from my room and not come out until I hear you in the kitchen, this time I don't know what to do or where to begin. I'm in the hall as you hang up your coat and your sweater, and I'm at the open bathroom door as you wash up, scrubbing a day's grime from your forearms and hands as the hot water blasts into the sink, soaping up your face, and finally cupping your hands together under the tap and sloshing the water into your face to wash all the soap away.

"Aaah!" You have taken an audible breath after swallowing the first spoonful of the steaming soup and I remember you had just torn off a piece from a slice of rye bread at the moment the story come tumbling out, all akimbo. As I cry and peer into your face, there is something new, a discomfiting fixity in your eyes; it is the first time I actually am conscious of anyone, of any adult—of you, giving me your full attention. I have only one question on my mind.

"Why, Daddy?" I ask, but burst into another sobbing spasm before you can say anything more than, "Don't worry. There's nothing to worry about now." You shake your head as I ask again and again: "Why, Daddy?"

"Why?" you say, eyes shining, gazing at me. "He wants to know why." You gesture outward with your right arm, hand relaxed, palm upward, the piece of bread still held between your fingers, your glance looking out above my shoulder and upwards. (It is a replica of the gesture you are making right now.) Then you stumblingly begin, "Oh, *mein kind,* my child, we're Jewish and…"

"No, no, no! That's not what I meant." You missed the whole point. "I know why they wanted to beat us up. What I want to know is why everybody ran away… Why Donny ran away… Why they left me there like that." I sob so hard I can't get any more words out.

You sit, the bread still in your hand, the soup still steaming. You fold your arms and gazed downward for a while, and then you look up. A strange tight smile flickers on your face, and you shake your head slowly. "That question also I could answer the same way, my child. You see, we're Jewish, and what Jewish people do is…they run." Suddenly the words are coming very fast and you too are crying. "But you didn't run, did you, *mein kind,* you fought them like a wild animal, they ran away, your friends, Donny and the rest, and left you, but you didn't run, my little American, my little Israeli."

Those words mystified me. Israel was nothing more than a map and trees to me in those days. It's true that, thanks to you, I knew the map of Israel as well as I knew the map of America, but none of us had ever even been to Israel.

"No, you didn't run," you said, still crying. "And I'll tell you one thing, those anti-Semite punks will remember they had a fight today, won't they." Your tears and your words frightened and bewildered me. "Come here, my boy."

I walked around the table, you pushed your chair back, and I sat down on your lap for the first time since I was really little. Do you remember how tightly you hugged me? I remember you said, "Yes, yes, there are new things under the sun."

That was the second time I saw you cry.

August 1952

HE WAS THERE ONE MORNING when I woke up early, at the enormous Victorian rooming house we were staying in near the beach,. He looked older than you, a little shorter than you and twenty or thirty pounds heavier, a solid, stocky man. . He spoke mostly in Yiddish. To my delight, the occasional English he used was articulately British. You told me he was from your hometown. His eyes were funny, sometimes twinkling good-naturedly, sometimes dead, sometimes with a terrible irony that mystified me.

He didn't towel himself off when he came out of the ocean or when he took an outdoor shower. He loved to let the water dry at its own rate. "It's refreshing, you know," he confided to me, trying to win me over. But I played hard to get, I don't know why. With Mother he was quite formal and polite, even a little diffident. But it was you he was here to see.

And how you two talked! Up and down the long hot day. I knew something was up when you set out with him on that walk in the middle of the afternoon, because you were wearing only your bathing suit and your floppy hat. Nothing protected your pale skin from the sun, and what made it even more unusual was there was no "Harry, watch yourself, you'll get a burn," or even a glance and a sign from Mother as you walked off with the stranger, your robe draped messily on your beach chair.

Later I'm sitting at the bottom of the stairs leading up to our room where you two are still talking, not making out the words though, even as a kid, I can discern the quiet intensity in your tone. Then you're shouting questions, then commands, and his voice becomes so faint I can barely hear it. The door flies open and crashes against the wall. He lunges out first, then you, and you're saying, *Ich farshteyt gantz gut,* I understand very well. *Ich kennit dus farleiden,* I can't bear it. And you have tears in your eyes. It terrifies me. You seem half in fury and half in anguish, and I hang back as you shove him down the stairs.

When I finally gather the nerve to drag myself to the porch, you are pushing him, past old Mr. Charnick sitting at the big poker table, down at the far end of the porch. The guy is making this weird keening sound that takes my breath away. I call out, but you don't turn. I run back inside , sit on the stairs and starting sobbing, I don't know why.

It was at least twenty minutes later when I slowly went out to the porch again. Old Mr. Charnick still sat there in one of the big wicker armchairs, tapping his loose-fisted right hand on the table in front of him, mumbling, "Again, it's me, only me they keep waiting," closing his fist and snapping the ring on his pinkie knuckle sharply against the Formica surface. "And card players they call themselves," he was saying, when the one everyone called Bluestone, the only one of the men you seemed to have anything to do with away from the card table, came in and sat down. I crouched down between the porch rail and the wicker sofa, one of my favorite hiding places.

"Such a commotion!" Charnick said. "And you just missed the whole thing. First, inside, someone's crashing down the stairs, not falling, but jumping four, five steps at a time, is what it sounded like.

And hollering in Yiddish! And a body smacking hard against something!

"Harry says, *To me you're the Angel of Death,* the *malakh hamovess.* No. No!

"Then the two of them come flying out right onto the porch. Harry and that hairy guy who was nosing around before, English, he sounded, asking about Harry and his family. The guy with the crazy eyes, they wouldn't keep still. The rest of him looked like it was made of rock, I'm telling you. But those eyes are something else. And Harry's crying and shoving him all along the length of the porch. The guy keeps turning and Harry keeps shoving him. And then in the middle the kid comes out, and he's whining *daddy daddy* as Harry keeps pushing the guy down the porch stairs to the street, and all the time the guy is making this high sound like a sick cat and he winds up on his hands and knees on the sidewalk–I got up and leaned over to get a good look–and he's on one knee looking up at Harry and then he got up and started backing away and turned around and then he's gone and it's over."

"So?" says Bluestone.

I peer over the sofa. The two of them are staring at each other, and I know that what I'm about to hear is the most important thing in the world.

"So, you're asking, and I'm telling. So Harry sits down right where you're sitting and you can see he's been crying . And you know, we're not that close, and I ain't sure I want to hear what he's gonna tell me, but his eyes are so wild, not like the other guy, but, for him, I'm saying. I keep my trap shut, and I get the whole story. The guy—and Harry never says his name–every time the name is coming out, you know, in a normal sort of way, Harry changes it to 'he' or 'him' like the name is burning his tongue. It turns out the guy was a good friend of Harry's big brother Mottek, back in Poland, in a city called Sambor. All of them, the brother, Harry, the guy, were *machers* in the Zionist club in the town. It was the first I heard of it. About things like that, he ain't a big talker."

"So?"

"So, again? Just listen. It was in '41, I think, and the Russians had pulled out and the Germans were coming. Harry had already left, in the thirties, and some *goyim* hid their sister in Vienna the whole time. But his brother, this Mottek, stayed back with his wife and two boys. And this guy, this same guy, comes to Mottek and says, *Let's go! We gotta get out of here.*

"And Mottek says, *Right you are! I'll get the wife and the boys and I'll meet you and Chana and Sheyndl*–Harry did say those names–*and we'll get out.* He asked the guy to give him an hour, I think."

"And the guy says to Mottek, *No, you don't get it. It's you and me, and it's right now, or we're all dead.*"

"And Mottek said no," says Bluestone.

"And Mottek said no."

"And Harry tells you all this."

"And Harry tells me all this. And the guy got away and has been living in Israel and has a new wife and a boy and a girl and all the rest were lost. A sister, and cousins. All of them. *Some nerve,* Harry says to me. *And he tells me he was in the battle for Jerusalem in '48. What the hell am I supposed to do with that tasty tidbit,* the oysvorf."

"Ah, brilliant," Bluestone says, more to himself than to Charnick, "He had to know Harry would have given anything to have been there. But let me get this right. You're telling me he came all the way from Israel just to tell to Harry the story about his brother Mottek?"

"That's what I'm telling you, exactly."

"And he also let it drop that he fought in the war in '48?"

"I guess so."

"The poor bastard," says Bluestone.

"You're right. It's too bad for Harry. Never in my life have I seen a man so wild looking, an animal, he was jumping and skipping and stopping, not like a regular person, running like that, the first time in my life I saw something like that."

"That's true," says Bluestone, "I believe you. But it's the other one I was thinking about just now. The both of them. The poor bastards."

I REMEMBER QUIETLY SNEAKING OUT from my hideout and tiptoeing up the stairs, then turning around and racing down the stairs and past the two of them who called out to me as I jumped off the porch. I caught sight of you, coming back, not from the beach but from

41

the other direction where there were blocks of overgrown lots, grass up to my shoulders, where all the kids played ringolevio and caught grasshoppers and cicadas and praying mantises late into the hot summer nights.

I sneaked a look at your face, then looked down and said, "Daddy, take me for a swim."

"Not now." Your voice sounded a lot calmer.

So this was not only the first time I saw you cry, it was the only time you ever turned me down, about a swim, that is.

September 1977

It isn't until I bring you and Mother back to the States six weeks after the stroke, that the reality of it sinks in, or, rather, that I sink into the reality of it. Language has been shattered for good. The little tidbits of language or comprehension, in writing and speaking, that gave us so much hope in the beginning have ended entirely, like the streams formed from mountain snow trickling to dryness by summer's end. The doctors are unanimous: there is no hope for verbal communication outward and virtually none for comprehension, and this condition will in all likelihood persist for years. On occasion your rage blazes up for a moment, as does the sadness and the weeping. And incredible remorse after the outbursts and fist shaking.

The strangest thing is the way you filled the days just before leaving Israel with affection for me, in your eyes, your gestures, your grabbing hold of my arm. I felt particularly close to you then.

It's hard to believe that just four months earlier–I had finally received my degree, (do you remember?)– I drove you and Mother out to the Catskills, first to a run-down bungalow colony, packed with wealthy observant wives from Borough Park and Crown Heights and their tribes of children, spending their summers as their immigrant mothers had. Not a place for the likes of you. Then another colony, with a few bungalows scattered on a huge thick manicured lawn.

And a small pool.

You immediately go down to the water and get in. I walk over and I'm watching you. I haven't changed into a bathing suit yet, and as I watch, I remember those Wednesday night suppers, Mother playing mah jongg with the "girls," me doing my job, eating with you or just sitting with you to slow you down, to watch you. You push off the side of the pool and slowly breast stroke across the pool towards me. I feel my heart beating. An old coagulated part of me wants to say something, to remind you about your heart condition. I don't, though. You reach my side of the pool in maybe five strokes. You turn and start back. I watch your arms move through the water, your head higher than in the sea–you're not fond of chlorine. You're moving easily. You pause and start back across. One. Glide. Two. Glide. I walk around and watch you reach the other side again, swimming right at me. You turn as if to start back again. You change your mind, rest there for a moment and come up out of the water, breathing just a little quickly.

You smile at me. You know your limits. You always have. I smile as you grab the towel, rub your chest, put on your glasses. We start walking through the grass. I see it now in my memory as if I were a camera, tracking along behind us as we walk. I see your crumpled gray bathing suit, your thin legs, pale skin, your powerful forearms and back and your sloped shoulders. I'm thin, a little taller.

A start! Your foot hits something. A pebble. You recover your balance in a step or two like a dancer. You wrap your left arm around my shoulders, hop up on one foot, and brush the pebble away. We resume walking. You leave your arm where it is as we walk in silence back to the bungalow.

Baseball

I never played catch with my father, nor soccer,
never saw him don a baseball glove or cap
though he'd sometimes appear on the sidelines

on the vast black parking lot that glistened in the July heat
to watch my big brother and his crew of high school
juniors and seniors in the fast pitch

softball games they wagered on
against other Rockaway neighborhoods
up and down the beaches Sunday mornings.

The arcana of baseball baffled
and amused him, but put a bat in his hand,
give him a few pointers

about stance and grip and so on,
and just try to fling the ball by him
at forty feet! Fat chance. But soccer

was his star sport in his teens
and early twenties, in Poland, a proper noun
that never crossed his lips in my hearing

save one weekend sixty years ago
when he took me to Randall's Island,
I in college, he in his fifties, to see Poland,

to his enormous pleasure, get thrashed,
two games in a row, by Pelé and Brazil.
"How come you never taught me soccer?" I asked

to the tune of one more felicitous feint by Pelé. "This is America," is what he said. "Baseball. Baseball." I've never seen him happier.

Wind Hair

> *Memory is a kind of accomplishment.*
> —William Carlos Williams, "The Descent"

To look at a recent photo of a daughter
and not to forget how for instance

thirty years ago her hair dryer in an instant
became a hand-held microphone
in the grasp of a teenage rocker;

to see her five-year-old daughter attentive
to every object–insects, glittering shards of glass, odd faces–
on the way home from school and not to forget

a second daughter that age walking home with her skinny pal,
the two of them leaning over, heads bent together, absorbed in the
    details
of some tiny form, like two old ladies or scientists;

to see a baby riding her father's back
hard in a carrier, trying to fly, and not to forget

a third daughter thrusting outward and up
against the seatbelt of the stroller
on our daily excursions as far as Nobscot
in absolute refusal of hat or hood
in any weather. "Wind hair! Wind hair!"
her pleasure and command
if I dared slacken the pace;

to feel a wintry anger possess me
now and not to forget how I learned when I

was five, to lie low when the fury of my father
swept by me as it chased my big brother
on the street, *talit* flying,

or, years later, how I learned
to turn memory into a sieve,
holding, relinquishing,
when similar rages
bubble up in me.

Opera

Sometimes, when I think of my father's last
seven years, his language so shattered I remember
only three occasions when I even suspected I could read
his desire, I find myself adrift....

if time were not inexorable....

and we'd known to call in a music therapist
who might have nurtured his brain
enough to make him one of those rare
stroke survivors able to sing
if not speak his desires to the tune of

Non più andrai, for instance, or *Là ci darem la mano,*
which he loved (and he stands before me, alive, now,
right hand cupped open, relaxed,
his first finger pointing upward, his pale clear eyes
and the tilt of his head steering us
toward the record player as he tried once again
to induce us to hear the beauty of some small inflection
in Pinza's rendering of the song) and as I look up
from my notebook, I can almost hear
his baritone, crooning,
Bring me some coffee, Bella.

But your art therapy studies wouldn't begin until four years
later and, no, never would he sing his desires,
and, as for music, hearing it, being comforted by it:
by the end he couldn't even bear
to listen to Jussi Bjorling, even with the volume

turned way down, hitting the soul
piercing final notes of "Nessun dorma":

vincerò, vin-ce-

rò.

The Merit of Ancestors

Try to Remember

Try to remember moments you can't know.
Not just the long slow summers
at the beach. The high rolling waves you rode. The sand crabs' nips.
The time your mother took you to see
Jack Kennedy, hatless in the bitter wind
coming in off the East River as he leaned
over the five-foot-tall labor leader
and warmed the old man's hand in both of his,
hair on fire in the bright winter sun.

You should remember moments you can't know.
Not just your father speeding through the Seder,
your mother's off-key voice that cracked
as she tried in vain—every year without fail—
to reproduce her father's *nigun* for the closing song:
Chasal siddur Pesakh kehilkhato

You must remember moments you can't know.
More than the conversations that swerved into rapid-fire Yiddish
when you came into the living room, though you did make out
some of the hushed names and words: Mottek, Rivka, pogrom, lager.

Remember the moments you can't know.
The murders, a few months apart, of your great-grandfather
and your grandfather along with two hundred thousand other Jews
in the Ukraine and Poland twenty-six years
before you were born. The way your grandfather
used to look up from his Talmud, walk over to his open study window,
stand there as your mother bounced her ball in the yard just outside,
and count every bounce.

Jewcap

        after Tomas Tranströmer's "Solitude-1"

I was anonymous
like a schoolboy in a lot surrounded by enemies.

Or not anonymous
so much as invisible

like Ellison's man
in a hole with a thousand incandescent lights.

Or like me, age nine,
South Eighth Street,
Brooklyn, after school,
Raymond Duffy, age thirteen, in my face.
"Take your Jewcap off," he's saying,
"I don't wanna insult your religion,"
and punching me so hard in the mouth, the curb
cracked into the back of my skull
before I could part my lips to answer back.

Not entirely unlike my Uncle Mottek
standing in the old Sambor graveyard
forced not to look away as they gunned down
his sons and then his wife
before forcing him forward,
to the piles of dirt, the common grave,
and the shovels, alongside
the other fathers, brothers, and sons,
in a new and final brotherhood:
burying their dead.

What My Mother Revealed

Every Friday morning the slaughterers'
collective would gather in my grandfather's
study and place the week's earnings
in assorted currencies on the large table,

where, from the time she was eight,
my mother, his youngest, would count out
the shares as her father beamed at her
from the head of the table, where,
other days, he'd pore over his Talmud.

A couple of years later, when she
eyed him from her position
on the floor of his study, distracted from her math homework
by having glimpsed
a classmate being beaten by his father
as she'd passed his house after school,

in answer to her question he wove a long tale
about the one time his own father struck him,
when he was ten, as she was then–he had climbed
a rickety fence to spy on the Bratzlaver Hassidim
who'd descend on their town, Uman,
for the entire month of the holy season
to lament, beseech, fast, and sing
wordless melodies at the grave of their leader,
this abandonment of family in the holy season
a topic of derision and gossip among
the native Jews of Uman. The boy
came upon an empty square,

a ramshackle grill, curling smoke, and spitting fat,
a slab of beef so huge it was probably meant to feed
the entire teeming hoard who'd left their wives and kids.
"I tipped it over," he said
exuberantly, having raced home with the news.
"The beef crashed down, oil and dust everywhere!"
"Oh! No!" The father raised his arm and smacked
his son downward across the face,
so hard he knocked him to the ground.

"It's a *shanda*, a great wrong you've done,
my boy," he said, lifting the son to his feet.
"Whatever we say about them inside our home—
and now I discern my own fault in this matter,
and your mother's—you must never forget
they too are Jews, they are human beings,
like us." Abstracted, he shook his head
slowly from side to side, wrapped the boy in his arms.
"Now, my child, I must, now, I must
go out to them. I must deal with this,"
and grabbed his hat and jacket and left.

What My Father Revealed

Of his mother
he never spoke. Of his father,

two facts and one action.
He owned a dairy
in their hometown in Poland.

He died of a stroke in 1933.

Once he happened to notice
the embroidered *parochet*

the curtain covering the ark in his *shul*
was frayed at its edges,
and he replaced it with one

more beautiful
which he had ordered
secretly and put in place

secretly. Though my father
had reread the tales of
Tevye der milkhiker in Yiddish

for decades and he'd sigh, a tender smile
fraying his pale blue eyes, as he spoke
of Tevye's daughters and their father, tiny

upheavals and huge ones, never was there
any slippage between
the fictional dairyman and the dairyman
he actually knew
as well as one son knew one father.

Ceremony

Though he would live
another six years,
one of the last times
my father made himself clear
was on the first Thanksgiving

after the stroke, with only family
present, the nine of us standing,
crowding the living room
turned dining room of my brother's
four-room apartment, he in his wheelchair.
It was the first time he met
my stepdaughters, aged ten and six.
What I remember is how busy he was
with them and my eight-year-old niece
for a long time, gesturing at them
and at the rest of us milling around him,
pointing, beckoning, his frustration slowly
sharpening as none of us, not me, not
my mother or brother, nor either
of our wives, managed to decipher
just what it was he was after,
his language having been shattered
entirely, leaving any hope of certainty
shattered as well—we weren't even sure
he grasped that I had married. Persisting,
attention now entirely on the girls,
my father eventually
got the three side by side
facing him, and then, by touch
and gesture, as they
seemed to be catching on,
fine-tuned the arrangement
until they stood left to right,
youngest to oldest, and his eyes,
panning slowly, met theirs,
one girl at a time, and then he reached out
wide, wrapped all three in his arms,

and drew them in, smiling, then shaking his head
familiarly in what had to have been
dismay and amusement at the alacrity
of the kids and the density
of the burdened grownups,
as the family at once became one.

My Father Speaks

Deuteronomy 6:4-7

You have forgotten me. The claim you're fond of–
that you think of me every day when you shave–
what sort of remembrance is that?

In your prayers you murmur the wish
I rest in peace–peace from what? Are you remembering
my chronic rages, as vague to me now

as the fine sleet of winter? Or is it only
an odd sense of proper manners, as if
you really believed in prayer? Better

to speak about me to your grandchildren
in the evening and the morning–
that might calm the restlessness I feel

that has only grown sharper
in this shadowy place, or, even
better, to remember when I could still

swim out beyond the jetties, with you
on my back, your little nails scratching
the skin over my collarbones

as you clung to me in fright and glee
with all your heart and all your might.
Best of all, swim out beyond

whatever breakers hold you back, now,
think of me, and do not be afraid.

II. Dreams of a Black Panther

Valentine 2014

Song of Songs 7:1-4

Yes, the flesh does hang differently
at seventy than it did when we met
decades back on the beach
in Herzliya, you lithe
in blue bikini, I in a baggy
green bathing suit, thickly bearded
with a tangle of dark hair,

yes, you caught your foot between rock and root
and broke your ankle at the end of our
hike in Austria in September,
and I caught mine on a post outside the library
two weeks ago and fractured three ribs,
and, yes, the imagination takes far more coaxing
than it used to at easel or desk,

but, still, we will manage to maneuver
down the sleet coated driveway in an hour
to get you to the doctor on time,

four-and-a-half-year-old Roni
did demonstrate to us this morning
on Skype from Tel-Aviv
that she will be Queen of the Night
on Purim this year by showing us her shiny black shoes
and hitting the high notes
of the famous aria, her mouth a perfect O,

and whether stumbling in crevices
or graceful in sandals, there is not a foot in the world
I'd rather massage at night, Love,
than yours.

Cinderella

You need another wedding dress, my daughter,
for the August heat of Israel, so you're in the TJMaxx
dressing room, trying a simple pale gray gown
that hangs on your body, your mother will say
later, with the line of archaic statues of Artemis,

and hisses of whispers lift up your eyes and turn them
from the full-length mirror to a pair of three-year-old girls
and their mothers, there, standing at the far end
of the room, and you can just discern
one of the mothers saying, "Well,

you'll just have to ask her," as both
of the women lightly nudge their daughters
forward, towards you, and the two girls approach
and ask, "Are you Cinderella?"
as one of the mothers mouths,
"Say yes," which you do.

Basketball

Genesis 28:16

At twenty-eight she has cast
a clear eye on basketball for the first time
and to her delight, caught on.

She dreams a little and happens to remember
how lost she had felt at the end
of an hour at a dig in Israel last year,
seeing nothing but sand and rubble
while all around her the others
kept spotting pale archaic shards,
until suddenly she found herself
in a liminal space in the sun-dazzle
in which each fragment of pottery cast
its own pale coral glow,
as if some god were in that place, holy.

So now a perfect pick and roll, KG closing
for the hole, unfolds slow motion
for her with the same lucent
clarity as those numinous shards, two
instances of perishable bliss: two spells cast,
in space, in time, they are visions for her,

not fantasy, she so into it now she dreamt
of Big Baby and Rondo the other night, wholly
unselfconscious and wholly amused
by the ambiguous undulations of her mind.

At Capo Vaticano

It came in quietly and in pieces, and left
the same way: the news: Martin saying they'd cut short
the plans to climb the rocks at the southern end
of our little cove and dive,

that Lyla had slipped and fallen in. She,
my oldest granddaughter, only eleven, had trailed the older girls.
A couple of hours later on the terrace upstairs,
she hovers, the thick coils of her long dark hair
covering my elbow, her blue eyes
enormous as ever: "What are you writing, Papa?"
And I, evasive: "About here."

Because Heimo, her uncle,
had arrived a few minutes after Martin
with the details. She'd slipped on a rock, fallen hard, head first,
Heimo, *bemikreh*, just happened
to be right behind her,
grabbed her by the foot, couldn't keep her
from going under, but kept her from smashing
her head and pulled her out. "Maybe she
hurt her head a little. She was brave, very
brave." Then Lyla herself arrived,
plopped down on the sofa with her father
and talking up a storm (I, too far away to hear)
they ended in a melody of teasing banter and laughter.
So in the midst of this tangled skein,
of family, grandparents, two daughters,
two husbands, brothers- and sisters-in-law,
cousins and a friend, a fact:
Heimo saved Lyla's life
perhaps. It's easy for me to imagine what Dani

must have been thinking,
given his prickly and cordial relationship
with his brother-in-law,
and the helplessness of not having been there,
as you and I hadn't been there twenty-four years back,
camping at Mount Greylock with another family.
We took a rowboat out on the lake,
the two of us alone out there,
with no thought at all to leaving Becca–
so sturdy and fearless, playing on the shore
with the couple's daughter, and her parents…

We learned from the children on our return
that Becca, no swimmer yet, got in over her head
and slipped off her float
while her friend dogpaddled along,
and was pulled out of the lake
by someone we have never met,
a stranger no one noticed,
"an *ish*," I couldn't help thinking,
who vanished; and twenty-four years later
I am still wondering, "What does mortal danger
really look like?" *Ish.*
Ish. And I am sweating a lot by now,
remembering those occasions in Genesis
when an *ish,* that is, a "man," appears–
or *anashim,* that is, "men," appear–
to be wrestled with, to bring tidings,
to intervene at the crux of a tale,
almost always carrying a trace
or an aura of divinity.

An intervention. A couple of hours later
on the terrace upstairs, looking out at the glassy sea,
catching the faint wisps of smoking Stromboli
in the distance against a heavy blue sky, Lyla
in serious conversation with Gabi and Dani
around the wire table below,
as Roni sleeps in their room and Hedi showers,
Heimo and Louis returned to the beach,
I remember the sister-in-law's words a couple of days ago:
how lucky we all are to have made it to thirty
and a wild anxiety rises in my chest
at this, the writing down
of even the faintest intimation
of losing a grandchild.

Ish, Ish, I whisper, *Anashim,*
Let the world be filled with *anashim!*

My Daughter

My daughter who is "overprotective"
according to her eight-year-old son.
My daughter who, at four, would descend into forty-minute tantrums
her only means of negotiating the rift
between two languages, two nations, two fathers.

My daughter who seemed tiny, a small mound
on a large hospital bed at twenty-five, in a tangle
of tubes and wires, four antibiotics
pumping into her body, when they finally
got it right, just after her appendix burst.

My daughter with eyes of blue sapphire.
My daughter who walks like a dancer.
My daughter who lives in the old chaos of toys and dishes,
bedclothes and papers, on a day of
everything at once.

Asphaltene

As I try to extract anything
from her pain and I fumble to distill
a precipitate of meaning from the sharp pang
when it came to her she had not been seen
by him for years, I am abstracted,
and thoughts hang there in my mind
the way Cezanne's apples are poised to roll down
and off the two-dimensional canvas or color
drips downward after a paintbrush
saturated with gouache is swept across
the top of a sheet of watercolor paper. Or I could
do a reverse and begin with the *finibus
graves rerum,* the heavy end of things,
after tears have dried or evaporated,
leaving only asphaltene, a suddenly solidified
and shapely hunk of glistening black liquid,
beautiful, carcinogenic. It is simply too much for me.

Forty-Five Years Ago

Psalms 38:6, 13–14

Yet another hazy grad school
party, late, our host asleep
on his back on the living room floor
again as music reverberates and the rest of us
dance or pick our way around him
laughing, drinking, smoking, and I've
come to a stop in the kitchen
doorway and there's his wife,
beautiful in profile, she
always the solidest of us
all, the one searched out when
drugs threw us off keel or our latest
love affair went awry into
heartbreak, there she was
in profile, still, slightly twisted
and bent, staring at the wall
over the sink, unable to hear
or make a sound, and the only word
that comes to mind now is "stricken," as tears
streamed down her cheek, and I
slipped back through the doorway
into the din of the party, her husband still
passed out on the floor, and I…willfully
innocent, I realize only now:
Intruder, not friend. Coward.

The Widower

> — *for Bulli*

I sit up in bed wakened by the snap
and sharp scrape of branches,
window rattling
in a long wind, like taking
a first sip of coffee and it's
salt, and was I the one
who put salt in the sugar bowl?

On the other side of the bed the sheet
is chilly, like the loud and distant moan
of the train whistle at the crossing
downtown.

I understand this feeling
is here to stay, like my oversized gray sweater
she loved to wrap herself in,
reading in bed winter nights,
like the smell of old wool, like the trace
still there of her Sicilian cologne.

Recognitions

Genesis 37:32, 38:25, 42:8

*The voice is the voice of Jacob,
but the hands are the hands of Esau.*

Genesis 27:22

I happened to be standing there, against the side rail,
facing the stairs to our friends' back porch, with Arnie
to my right along the back rail, as his mother
came in, looked right at me, and said, in her
emphatic voice with its familiar jocularity,
"Hello, Ar-nold," and my eyes turning
caught Arnie's, welling up, and too many feelings–
anguish, irony, sheepishness, and something
like a stoic shrug–rose up, flickered,
and flitted about his face, between
the not-quite-smile on his lips
and those eyes. Yes, my friend, that's how it is,
he didn't have to say as he followed her
into the house and my hand squeezed his shoulder
as he passed and I entered behind him
to you, my Love, your eyes searching
my face. "What is it, Bernie?"
you're saying softly. "What's wrong?"

The Dinner

Our first dinner together:
six parents of teenagers, each couple,
it turned out, having been carrying
the amazed conviction that all the others
had somehow mastered this parenting business,
until one of the fathers said,
across platters of steamed fish,
Szechuan green beans, family style
eggplant, and vegetarian moo shi,
"Let me tell what happened this morning,"
with a seriousness that nudged
the cacophony of overlapping conversations
into silence. "All I said to her was,
'How are you doing?' To which she replied.
'What did you say that for?'" And all six of us
at once were getting words in edgewise in a flood of revelation
of how comforted we all had been
by the belief that anyone had it down,
this labor of parenting, how we all
were grappling in uncertainty
at the stunning opacity of it all,
that has not let up much
over almost four decades of dinners.
Meryl. Bob. Arnie. Lorel. Bernie. Linda.

At the Movies

Why do the words spoken by the man,
who drifts in isolate silence from scene
to scene and erupts in intermittent rages,
get to us? Why do the words
spoken by the man, who'd lost
three adored children ten years earlier
in a fire he had caused
in drunken carelessness and muddiness
of thought, catch us in the region
of the throat? His ex-wife, a new mother
now, having run into him on the street,
broke down in gulping sobs
as she told him she regrets her cruel words
to him all those years ago (words we never hear)–
her heart will always be broken,
she tells him, as will his.
"I love you," she tells him, whispering,
"could we ever have lunch?"
This is the man who can't
stand still as she speaks,
bobbing and weaving as if her words
fly at him like boulders. "I can't beat it,"
he says finally, "I just can't
beat it," in a clarity of comprehending
the impassable abyss between
intention and impact, remorse
and consequence. Ashamed, he finds himself
entirely irredeemable, and he does not shy away.
And it gets to us, that stolid
willingness to face the old truth
that *even in our sleep, pain that cannot forget*
falls drop by drop upon the heart.

After the Rehearsal

for Danny

"Impossible," he said once more. "Exit,
pursued by a bear" (shaking his head).

"No more impossible," I said,
"than the miracle that ends the . . ."
As usual he waves my words aside
and says, "It also is a play in which
a man can catch a vicious strain of jealousy
the way you catch a cold."

I'd been watching the *Macbeth* rehearsal
for a couple of hours,
as he'd coaxed Barry-as-Macbeth toward
a Hamlet-like attending to every movement

of the villain's mind, alert to every line,
surprised, perplexed, sometimes
even baffled at everything he thought and did
(and didn't do) as he spoke the almost too
familiar words. "Tomorrow and tomorrow...."

A couple of weeks later: the best *Macbeth* I've ever seen.

Afterwards, I, neither playwright nor director,
am at him again about *A Winter's Tale*
"It's time you took it on."
He laughs, entirely amused.
"It really is impossible, you know.
I haven't even mentioned the pastoral
stuff, or stuffing, one might say." "It's all

the same," I say, "the jealousy, the bear,
the miracle. It's all, all about wonder," I say,
"and what tops that?" He smirks, still amused,

and it's a cinch to picture us sitting side by side
outside somewhere in Adirondack chairs when we are eighty.
"Miracle," I growl. "Impossible," he croons.

Sappho's Blues: Four Songs

1

Goddess, hear my plea--
this time I'm speaking for myself alone—
please relieve my pain.
My heart is crushed with agony.
Please come to me from your dappled throne.
Goddess, don't delay.

Remember the time
you yoked your thick-winged horses
and rode them down to my dark room.
You were happy to show me
your ironic smile,
and said, "Darling Sappho, what's the trouble

that makes you call again?
Just name the fool who has treated you cruelly,
and I will bring her around.
Does she turn away?
Soon she'll come running with the love that is due you
a love that knows no bound."

You asked me then
what my poor heart most wanted
and did everything you could to end my grief.
Please come again,
give me what I most hope for,
fight right beside me.

Goddess hear my plea
fly down from the heavens to this dark earth again
and Goddess set me free.

2

Dear Goddess we are waiting
in your sacred grove alive with sound
where we whisper, "Aphrodite,
come now."

Leaves quiver in the moonlight
a rose thicket shades the ground
where we whisper, "Aphrodite,
come now."

Your favorite incense
is casting out its fragrance,
an enticing cadence
to taste and hear.
A bright spring murmurs
behind the apple branches,
it gleams and dances,
so cool and clear.

Sleek horses gallop lightly
through fields where poppies float like clouds
we croon, "Aphrodite,
come down."

O Goddess fill our cups up
until they overflow their brims
with love laced with your clear wine now.
Drop in!

The scent of dill

lingers in the salt air,
a mixture so rare,
it's hard to breathe.
Bewitched by incense,
poppies, leaves, and roses,
the whole night dozes,
pours down deep sleep.

Dear Goddess we are waiting
in your sacred grove alive with sound
where we keep praying, "Aphrodite,
come now."

O Goddess fill our cups up
until they overflow their brims
with wine laced with your hot love now.
Drop in.

3

Mother dear, I can't do the dishes
Or clean the tub after my bath.
Mother dear, I'm not being vicious.
I don't want to provoke your wrath.

Don't blame me, I can't help it!
Blame Aphrodite, soft Aphrodite
She has thrilled me with a wrenching joy!
Don't blame me, I can't help it!
Blame Aphrodite, soft Aphrodite
She has almost killed me with love for that boy.

Mother dear, I can't do my homework,
I can't even tell a circle from a square,

I practice my lines but my mind is murky,
My earthbound soul is made of air.

Don't blame me, I can't help it!
Blame Aphrodite, soft Aphrodite
She has thrilled me with a wrenching joy!
Don't blame me, I can't help it!
Blame Aphrodite, soft Aphrodite
She has almost killed me with love for that boy.

4

At noon when the earth
was bright with flaming
heat that dropped straight through my heart,
the crickets set up
a high pitched singing
that got me to play a quiet part,

I held my guitar
caressed it slowly
letting the strings
speak out about death.
If you'd join in
sing my words softly
you'd make me immortal
in your breath

Last night with his venom
as the moon and Orion
crawled on their journey down the sky
Last night sweet bitter
last night irresistible
last night as I lay on my bed alone,

Last night with his venom
cloaked in purple
Love so shyly wound around,
loosening my limbs
poisoning my spirit
Love that reptile struck me down

I grab my guitar
caress it slowly
letting the strings
speak out against death
Please join in.
Sing my words softly.
Make me immortal
in your breath.

"Easy Come"

"Good shot!" And we looked at each other
and laughed, according to the punch line
of a story we've told together or apart
so often it's a family saying.
How the stranger retrieved and held up
his small black ball and we,
brand new to each other,
spoke in unison. In English. "Good shot!"

I hadn't noticed the ball fly into the beach bag
of the blue-bikinied mother of two
who'd gone off to the kiosk
with her two girls for drinks. I had heard the flurry of invective
that poured out of her in Hebrew
as the stranger had reached into the bag
and held the ball up resting on three fingertips.

She had noticed me, too,
having heard me speaking loudly
in English or in American-accented Hebrew
at the rear of the beach-bound bus,
then seeing me alone on a towel not ten feet
from where she had settled with her daughters
at the far end of the beach. I thought her
an ideal Israeli mama.
She thought me an American academic.
"Easy come," I think. It's
thirty-eight years later.
Neither has gone.

In Provincetown

According to Mapquest it was 1.47 miles,
our night walk down Commercial Street
back from the restaurant at 321
to the motel at land's end in the splatter and wind
of the first nor'easter. Clenched

together, arm in arm in the cold,
the few streetlamps dimmed in the fine rain,
I falling out of step, repeatedly,
annoyingly, we were alert as we peered
through or between the thick hedges
along the way, guessing
is it this one or is it that
hiding the intricate array
of Stanley Kunitz's poetry garden.

Our large blue and white umbrella
was furled, useless in the exhilarating wind
    and the intermittent buckets of small rain
        flung at our faces from all directions, down
and up, the clean ocean air filling our noses
    and our lungs as we remembered

    the earlier walk in the opposite direction at the tail end of dusk in
        gusts and mist,
no rain, not a car in sight, our footfalls quietly thudding
    on the wet street,
and suddenly fading in: the rising and falling notes of an alto sax
    hanging above
and all around us,
    saturating the dark blue air, it seemed–

a couple of blocks later, there he was in the shadows, a lone musician
huddled in a doorway, folded over his sax,
singing out a noirish soundtrack for our lives.

Aubade: Wonderland

Half-asleep in the merry grays of predawn light,
the wall I sleep against on our granddaughter's bed

is soothing and cool in the warm
Tel-Aviv November morning.

At eye level
are the pinafore and dress of Tenniel's giant Alice
a yard high, rendered by our granddaughter in Sharpie:
a gift for herself between wake and dream;

I roll over carefully, and inches from my eyes
is your face—you're on your back, lips parted
slightly, the sound of your breath inaudible
even this close-up.

You look thirty,

your quiet breathing, slow,
            in
              and out,
like the swelling and easing of the Mediterranean
smooth and glistening as far
as the eye can see
baring her bosom to the sky
just before sunset yesterday,

the marks and wrinkles of your face
from so many decades of living in gravity somehow absorbed
into flesh in this moment as I am absorbed

until

    the first drip of sunlight pings your eyebrow,
you murmur something
undecipherable,
and I'm back
to my sole self and time, gone

the lying here
gazing at your face forever.

Dreams of a Black Panther

> *…I thought*
>
> *this was how one became*
> *a woman.…*
> *…*
> *What to do with this girl?*
>
> Rosanna Warren, "Ghost in a Red Hat"

The lettuce glows, green leaf, red leaf, romaine,
just planted amid chives which turned out to be
perennial, having to our surprise
survived record snows in the soft circular planter
a foot high and a yard in diameter
I had filled with topsoil last summer
near the green chain-link fence.

    At seventy-one I remember

trying to disappear in the darkness
under my first grade teacher's desk
where she imprisoned us for misdemeanors
I don't recall, and, a year later,
feeling the hard wooden shelf of the blackboard
press sharply into my shoulder blades
as my second grade teacher, his back to me,
ground his heels into my instep
whenever I spoke out of turn.

I tried to lie low, but was so besotted
with learning and performing what I'd learned
I kept speaking out of turn.

What to do with this boy?

He learned to perform what he'd learned for his parents
to secure their love.
He learned not to listen to others.
He learned to be afraid.

He dreamed of a black panther stalking prey in the night forest
and he was the panther in daydreams after he woke.

Years later he would wander alone by the Charles
along avenues of old sycamores, so large
and still they seemed inanimate,
as night gave way to transparent dawn,

or jog there other mornings and wind up
at the old Patisserie Français, a regular,
often sharing a table with the Lebanese owner.
They'd dip fresh croissants into strong café au lait,
and, negotiating hard, they'd settle, once and for all,
all the outstanding issues between Israel
and its neighbors, sealed by a promise to share
their personal Beiruts and Tel-Avivs
no later than the summer of 2000

—forty years ago
it was—those intense, hopeful,
bemused conversations were also
alluring for women,

with whom for many years he perfected asymmetry,
lovable to some, others

lovable to him, he learned that staying alone
was also a way of reaching out.

    Why did he attract so many he didn't love?
    Or did he not love them because
    he attracted them?

He wasn't bad at friendship,
but heartbreak…well…dispensing it,
nourishing his own. So much unnecessary pain.
Was that how one became a man?

He liked the fact that the heavy metals in our bodies—
copper, selenium, zinc—are created
when stars collide, back near the beginning
of time. He liked the fact
that he could trace his family back
two hundred years or so (at least
on his mother's side) to a now
notorious town in the Ukraine.

So steeped in snow this winter
were the suburbs where I live now
that more concrete facing than usual crumbled
off the stone wall along the driveway.
No matter how diligently or obsessively
the top of the soil had been cultivated
for vegetables, grass, and flowers,
the poor earth of our back and side yards
threw more rocks than usual
up to the surface, the forsythia
is scraggly, there's just a nub or two of tulip,

and the daffodils and crocuses
enter starkly one by one, absent
the crowds and hosts of other years,

But what? "Look," I told Linda, two days later, "there they are."
Luminous white and yellow trumpets
of daffodils, a calmer yellow gathering of lilies,
poised on their tall stalks, a smattering of grape hyacinth
scattered among a swarm of purple and white crocuses–
the deep snow obviously a good thing
for them–

and Linda told me this morning she'd seen
her first rabbit, so we'd better see
to protecting the lettuce she planted,
having called me downstairs
for asparagus, eggs,
and Pecorino Romano on toast
and a double latte.

III. Red Red

Any Misery in the Sound of the Wind

Its young ones suck up blood;
And where the slain are, there it is.

—Job 39

Or you're five and a half, and we're sitting in the garage
turned family room of the Wickford Street slab rental,
with the faux wood panels and the
brown shag carpet, and mama turtles on TV
lumber up from the sea to lay their eggs,
and babies
break through shell and sand and scurry
down the beach as fast
as their baby legs can go, and,
before I can even wonder, "Why the big rush,"
it's a long shot, and plummeting

like red-tailed hawks or dive bombers
is a skyful of wide-winged frigate birds, braking,
grabbing the babies in their talons, soaring, dashing
them on the rocks, and you're yelling,
tears flying from your face. "Why
(sobbing) don't they
do something?"
"Who?" I say.
"Them," you say,
"the people making the movie."

The Snorkelers

(after Whitman)

Unruly old vastness,
indifferent ocean,

I think I could spend my life
among the snorkelers, at the edge of
some reef in the Red Sea; they have only one
eagerness: to point out the latest specimen of stunning beauty
that swims into their ken.

They do not brawl or rage against injustice.
They do not dwell on pain, inflicted and received.
They do not think they are gods.

They don't regret the past or worship the past.
They don't drown the present in plans or worries,
hopes or dreams. They are not
respectable, but a few
old timers, remembering the reef
entirely free of leprous patches,
laconically remind us
this earth
is all we have.

Betrayal

is the slippery
underleaves along
a long familiar trail
in Callahan
late on a winter day,
your legs slipping out
from under you,
slamming you down
hard on your shoulder
blades, your body
sliding to a sharp
stop as your heels jam
against abrupt roots–
and yet,
flat on your soaking
back, abrasions
stinging the backs of your arms
and your legs, there they are
between tall leafless trees:
the first three stars
in the dark purple sky,
and gleaming,
floating,
it's Venus.

On Ahad Ha'am Street

Does the hawk fly by your wisdom?

Job 39:26

A pair of hummingbirds
darts around the living room
of this third floor apartment,
having flown in, as they do
every year at this time,
before they settle down and perch
on the wire braided with philodendron vines
Dani has strung along the high ceiling.
The eyes of Effie, framed by her
dark charcoal velvet coat,
seem all white, save the pinpoint black pupils
in her irises as she fixes them
in a glare and tiger-like
stalks them along the wall,
under the table, across
the light gray yoga mat,
and fixes on them again
directly over her head,
transfixed, and they rustle up
the ivy, twitter once, twice,
and flit, looping and somersaulting
in bravura virtuosity, perhaps,
onto the balcony, Effie following
Zen-like? poised to strike,
and now just out of reach
on a broad green leaf,
the two tiny creatures
chirp their heads off right at her.
a hummingbird rendition, I figure,

of *NA-na-NA-na-NAAA-na,*
then they take off
and the night has them.

Late December Nightfall

Genesis 15:11

We'd been sledding down the hill by the deaf school
all afternoon. Toward sunset we began
at the far end of the field, a snowman,
a real McCoy of a snowman, taller than I, three spheres
of perfect snow—you're sitting on my shoulders and reaching up
to bring the face to life and I look up and notice
it's the night end of dusk,
only the sky right above us still day.
I put you down, we're the only ones left, and cold is coming in hard
    on the wind,
you three and a half, plump in your puffy purple snow suit,
    rosy cheeked,
I taking hard cold breaths, then silence, then

hunhHUNH! hunhHUNH! hunhHUNH!
three Canada geese right above us, a leader and two wingmen,
fifteen feet from the ground, trumpeting,
gliding, the black brown white at full extension.
We don't move and the *whish whish whish* of the wings
breathes on our faces and your hand
goes up to your cheek to check, fearless,
but my heart is at my throat, my whole body
trembling in fear and something
else, as if these geese were birds of prey
and I were Abraham surrounded by animal carcasses
driving them off into another darkening sky.

You flap your arms slightly
just as you had last summer
when thousands of seagulls

rose as one in the cove below us
and soared above the California coast,
your eyes wide
wide in delight.

Laughable

It should be laughable, to leave a cabinet
door ajar once again or a drawer open and not
know why you did it or why you always forget
your intention always to cast a mental spot-

light all around a room before you leave, to protect
shins and heads, yours and others', from protruding
corners that you know too well should be tucked
in. You can't help wondering, "Is there anything

at all to this?" Is the child in you still abiding
in the aura of a doting mother who'd pick
up invisibly after you, silently sliding
drawers into chest, doors into jambs? No kick

for you at your age this carelessness, only disdain
for some vestigial need to mark your intimate domain.

Raccoon

Thud pad pad pad, dull crash.
The plastic garbage can gone over, it's too dark
just outside the bedroom window to see–
but I know who it is–
I remember last spring–we had been leaving
bowls of cat food outside the glass door
to the patio, and suddenly the cats were acting
ravenous every morning, David doing
the rolling-over-on-my-ankle trick I'd taught him
over and over, the bowls completely empty
save the black blotches that turned out to be
telltale. The next evening
you fill the bowls again in the dusk
and I, around midnight, look out from the dining room table.

Five. Chattering there.
I open the door and roar. Four
are up the oak in a hurry. The fifth,
huge, fat, hunkering, backing up slowly,
bares her teeth, protective. I step toward her.
She inches backward toward the tree, an arrow
pulled taut against a bowstring,
and our eyes meet and lock
in the indirect light of the dining room fixture.

When the gorilla in the Franklin Park Zoo
last summer was sitting at ease, his back resting against
the glass wall of the cave, some kids kept banging the glass
until he rolled his hominid yellow eyes and I thought,
for all the world, it could have been human,
that gesture, and I felt an infinite sadness in him,
in me, too, aching, in my desperate search for sense,

a sadness of slavery or imprisonment
of biology is destiny, of genes,
of instinct looking across the infinite abyss,
at my freedom, at his.

But as I look across
at this other creature with human hands,
five feet away, eye to eye,
my dread is absolute.
This staring raccoon who's shared my world
for two years at least is simply Other.
I gaze back at her, but what do I know?
I was not there
when the foundations of the world
were set.

Ankle

It's never had this much attention, this limb
of mine, the right ankle, to be exact, in a blue cast,
the fibula fractured neatly near its lower end.
When people ask, I kid around:
I was skiing in Chile? Digging holes
for lettuce in my terraced garden? You decide. Dream

or carelessness? You decide. For me it's abrupt
waking up from a bad dream, it's wrestling
with some shadowy figure. I'm far

too alert, the sorry limb
numb or achy, or, worse,
just there. I don't feel whole, I
can't hold on anything, this damn limb
of mine, my whole body with it, hovering

in and out of focus, a bit outside,
a bit inside my skin, at the very edges
of my perception, all around me.
Proprioceptively, too: inside
my body, nothing is whole,
as if at every moment
I'm way out on a limb.

I have become many.

Ridiculous, isn't it?
It's just a goddamned broken ankle,
I hear myself say out loud. Let it be…
as if in prayer…no, as if the words
were a spell-ending incantation
that would make me one again.

Above Leuk

Ezekiel 37:2-5

When the pile of hollow skulls and dry bones
was discovered one hundred years back
beneath the altar of the twelfth-century church
above Leuk, who got the job of heaping and shaping
the tangled chaos of human remains
to make the even inner walls
of a chapel? Did he do his building
as carefully and rapidly
as the master wall builders of Connecticut
our teacher told us about, who'd worked
mortarless, as they tossed stone rubble
from a cleared field perfectly
into place? Who taught him to throw in
an occasional femur here and there to make
the wall to ceiling construction entirely
self-supporting, each breathless skull, each dry bone,
holding all the others up so neatly and
economically if one shard gave way
in an instant we would find ourselves
buried as the bones were, waiting for centuries
among the crumbling remains?

What I Knew

In memoriam R. P. G. (1945-1994)

Razory, shrewd, at 3 a.m. in the poolroom
of our dorm, bugging and trouncing me,
as usual, he, not even able to raise his elbow
above his damaged shoulder.
                        He's at me,
needling and nailing his various trick shots
as I missed the long draws and scratched
on the gimmes, his stiletto banter
about pool, Bartok, and linear algebra
slicing up all of my ineptitudes.

                        Anyone
would have deemed it nasty
and simply too much by the time
I spoke up. "Why don't you go fuck
your sister," I said, "and leave me
the hell alone?"
                        and he's actually foundering
as he staggers backwards, bent over and gasping
as if I'd just socked him in the gut as hard as I could,
and he's staring right at me now, silent, elbowing
his way back out of the room, leaving me alone
there under the bright light fifty years ago, cursing

my freshman psych conviction that repression is universal
and wishing he hadn't told me of the long slow death
of his father at forty-nine and the pretty kid sister
who'd spent her fifteenth year every day
after school in the den turned sick room
attending the dying man alone,

her desperate mother working long hours,
her adored big brother away at college.

Before I spoke I didn't even know
what I knew.

Sycamores

In my thirties, on one of the long nights
of the year, I would stare out at the courtyard
of my red brick apartment house at three
in the morning–having been working
at my trestle desk for hours–and regularly,

my perfect Cambridge apartment suddenly
became uninhabitable. I never knew why.
But I'd throw on my winter coat, hat, and scarf, head
for the river, and make my eight-mile loop
along the Charles and its lights, eastward all the way

to the museum, across at the old dam,
back along Storrow, back across the frozen river
and up the great avenue of sycamores,
those great looming petrified hides
having become my own lilac blossoms of courage.

There I'd pause,
breathe the clear night air in deeply,
and realize my demons–
I never knew why–
once again had fled
the opaque cavern of my chest.

Red Red

Genesis 25:30

As I hoisted the last and heaviest
of the storage bins from the highest
shelf in the garage, it shifted, started to slip, my
heart jumped, and my hand got caught, skin
pinched between bin and shelf. I yowled,
and I laughed at my typical clumsiness
"Have a look," I said as you rushed
in, took in the wine red blister, and lifted it
to your mouth. *Is that all there is?*
I wondered as I looked at your blood-stained lips

On our first road trip with the girls
years back, the four of us getting so
under each other's skin after six hours in the car
we traded the highway for a country
road somewhere in Ontario, where we bought
quarts of raspberries–a rationed luxury
at home–at a roadside stand. We threw them
into our mouths by the handful, crushed the sweet
piquant capsules between palate and tongue,
gobbled them down, and couldn't stop laughing,
sputtering as we pointed–*is that all
there is?*–at our red-stained lips and teeth.

IV. The Ideal World

The Silence

for Joel

And around these, in a larger circle
of pain and time, two hospitals are scattered
and one graveyard.
Yehuda Amichai, "The Diameter of the Bomb"

In the silence last night I managed
to recapture my vision early in the morning of the second day
of a universe sopping with kindness that saturated the white space
    around me which contained
             the *sssss* and caress of breath in nostrils, cool and
warm,
cool in, warm out,
    cool in, along the top of the nose,
        warm out, along the bottom,
and the pale odor and ambiance of a hundred bodies breathing in a
    large room,
        and my faintly acrid tongue.

            In the silence,
I let my breath begin coolly in the intake through my nostrils
and slowly pour downward into the abdomen, then chest,
    swelling the lower ribs
        and the upper ribs outward and upward into a large
    spaciousness
            and then pause
and then empty from the top down
        warmly into the room where it joined all the others

breathing out and in in even breaths. In the silence I didn't stop there
but let the breath continue outward, all the way,

to the great domain of total peace where somehow,

slowly fading in, there was music, a new melody
for the old invocation: may the source of peace out there
let peace rain down in here,
on me, on my people, and on all who live on earth,

but in the silence it wasn't a prayer,
but a sensation that a moment later tangled up with a vision
of the debris of a terror bomb and the circle of death and grief
around it, that expands across oceans and continents,
and carries the cries of orphans outward and upward
to the end of all ends where there is no God
but only a larger silence.

Mind, Feel

Mind, feel, not only the books
you are immersed in,
not only how your thoughts riff
on available realities,
but also those times, stained
by the memories of a lost love
or fears of what you see coming,
how often you simply are not here.
Feel the texture of the pen
along your fingers and thumb,
and its scrape, feel, mind,
how the widening eyes
of your beloved
warm
the flesh of your face.

Strange Love

There I stood thriving in my arena,
a classroom that felt radical, dangerous, full
of voracious Vietnam vets
the spring after our poor nation again
picked Dick–and I'm on a roll doing *Strangelove*,

"Don't you see," I say, "don't you see
what Kubrick's up to?" A hand goes up.
"We are rooting for the plane to get through!"
More hands, and I, really slowly, quietly:
"We are rooting for the plane to get through."
A forest of hands. "Don't you get it? We are rooting
for the end of the world. We are rooting
for nuclear war." By now a few are shouting out.
"Why the hell not?" says one. "This fucking
country," says another, and someone
else says something else

twenty minutes to
go in the…
in the class and it's all slowly…
in a narrow…
and blurry,

and I manage to get out something like, "I'm sorry.
I can't go on now," and I walk out.

My hand
is at my throat, as if in that moment
nothing at all
could be "me," "my,"

other than the countless childhood performances
the only things the child in me
was sure his parents loved—

there, resisting any deviation, any attempt to turn
or change, is the inertial tonnage
of the huge beast that is my childhood.

The truth is, I have to say, I came out of this
a week and a half later, sitting
on an old splintery bench, my bench,
watching the sun go down
across the Charles as single sculls slid by:
somehow I managed to see myself again in that class,
conceding, yes, I belonged
there, conceding as well that my parents'
desires and terrible needs make only one strand
of the incalculable web of desire, choice,
and accident woven by me and a cast of thousands
that landed me in that classroom
at that time in that breakdown
that kept me from pressing them toward
the big idea that art can tell us
to change our lives, that morality can inhabit form
and beauty cry out for justice.

I did decide to listen more.

Schubert

"We're late bloomers," my friend Nolletti said
in the mid-nineties in one of our quick exchanges
in the hall, and what could I do but agree,
as I remembered the spring of '77, when I sat
and stared at the old man's watercolor
(a Lake District landscape painted from memory)
over the mantle in my Cambridge pad: I was touching
bottom then, broken by six long years
of heart and dissertation wars with myself
and others, face to face now for the first time,
with the truth next door to despair,
that I don't have to finish,
that It is not my mind, It is not
my parents' dreams, It is not perfect,
It will not change my life: It is itself,
no more, no less, and somehow, as alone
as I've ever been, I knew enough
to fill my eyes with the watercolor
and the room with Schubert,
the C Major quintet it was,
and my imagination dead,
I haunted Schubert, and he,
me, his heart, too, shaken
in the indescribable and exquisite feud
that mingled the tenderness,
joy, and grandeur he must have heard
with the dim-conceived glories
that filled his mind
before setting hand to piano,
pen to paper: the quintet too, only itself,
no more, no less.

Death, Rothko Said

"Death," Rothko wrote in his studio a few blocks from Radio City,
where the Rockettes kicked their way through my Jewish childhood
on Christmas and Easter, is one of the necessary
"ingredients" of a work of art–like the *malkosh*,
for instance, the special word in a desert country
for the last rain–death: the truth element
in his calculus of beauty. Wit: the human element–
a triangle constructed from
childhood stickball as night falls
on South Eighth Street, Brooklyn,
a six-year-old girl bringing mountain snow
home in a cup to her pal in a tropical city,
and a horseshoe crab on its back
at Rockaway Beach, all of its legs in motion–
is necessary, too, he said. As is chance, tension,
irony, hope, and "a lustful relationship
to things that exist." And memory—
I would add, a lifetime falling away
before my eyes a month ago at an inadvertent
return after nearly seventy years to McCarren Park Pool,
which closed time and again
from the polio scares of my childhood
summers—the second human element.
"When Ika died," my friend said two years ago,
as the mind drifted outward towards infinity.
"When Ika died," he said two months ago
on Skype, the phrase having become
the before and after of his life.

Hope. Heartbreak.

— for Kath

Felt in the blood, and felt along the heart
　　　　　William Wordsworth, "Lines Composed above Tintern Abbey"

"No. Not any of the poems you read
or spoke of today." I'd been a guest
at a friend's class in Tel-Aviv. Wrapped in a black hijab, wide
brown eyes luminous, it was
another poem she wanted to ask about,
one of mine she had tracked down
in her Galilee village on her Mac.

I couldn't recall her name yesterday when she came to mind–
as she often does

She'd spoken softly, after,
in perfect English, the faintest trace of accent
adding a lilt and a charming *tzlil*,
　　　　　　　　　　so softly
I had to lean close to her, as we walked
in the high atrium after class
through the rapid flow and quick glances
of her classmates around us.

She wanted to know why I'd written "robbing"
and not, for instance, "celebrating the gods"
about the "hour of love" I grabbed
"luxuriously in the late afternoon."

　　　　　　　Surprised
by her absorption, her attention,
the knowledge she had my poem by heart,

or something else entirely,

                I couldn't speak
for a moment as the two of us, alone now,
came to a stop in the long high corridor.
"Well," I said,
"I was attending to time, you see…"

"Ah." Her eyes turned from mine,
tilting a bit upward and to the side (and inward I realized)
"Yes," she murmured. "I do see. 'Hour'…'late afternoon'…
Time was there from the very first line."

And she's saying, "Thank you
for taking the time (a quick grin; a slow smile)
to talk to me."

And turned and walked away…
as *thank you* took form on my lips.

I think of yesterday's news—

an outbreak of internecine stabbings
all across Israel, dwelled on
in Israeli blogs and papers
(barely mentioned by the Times and CNN)
and poll results that showed if nearly half
of Jewish Israelis had their way, all
the Arabs, Moslem and
Christian, would be expelled—

remember her questions, picture her
walking off, and wonder, "Does she remember, too?"

And if she does remember now, after all that has happened
to her people, would she still ask such questions?
And with what judgments, what sensations?
Heartbreak? Anger at herself?
At me? Or *thoughts too deep for tears?*

He Rises: A Vision, January 2, 2020

Henry Bacon, architect, knew what he was doing, I tell myself
once again, as I approach the Memorial and lift my eyes to the broad
        staircase
rising to the enclosed statue of the great man
seated within his sanctuary.

By the time I reach the bottom of the stairs
he has vanished, the angle of ascent
too steep to keep him in view
and I ascend, small in the wide expanse.

Daniel Chester French, sculptor, also knew what he was doing–at the top
of the stairs, the statue fully visible again, my eyes are drawn to the right leg
poised forward as if about to stand, and irresistibly I yield to the vision
of the great man rising to his feet,

waking from his stony sleep
as babies of color are again being torn
from their mothers' arms a century and a half
after the great civil war,

Towering now, I imagine him gazing around the chamber
slowly, his deep stone eyes resting
for a moment on *equal*, on *liberty*, on *a new birth
of freedom*, on *binding up the nation's wounds*.

He turns. I close my eyes. I almost feel
the reverberation of long strides;
walls, floor, and ceiling trembling
as he crosses the room and descends.

A mile away, our prickly would-be emperor
squats naked in his mirrored room

toadlike, shameless, his cutters and trimmers
flitting around him.

Outside, the man of stone arrives. Behind the wrought iron fence
he speaks, Emoluments, he says. With charity for none,
you wring your bread from the sweat of other men's faces,
you tear apart the nation's wounds.

I open my eyes, his final words on my lips: You're through.

Five Consolations

   1.

Two messengers at the entrance before dawn
promise a fertile spring

   2.

and your name
voiced aloud by your beloved in a dream
softly wakes you at four a.m.

   3.

and a flock of crows
on a canvas, each one rendered
in two black strokes,
as a child might–descending
or ascending, they are buffeted
by a dark blue storm wind
that turns the wheat fields into rough ochre surf

   4.

and you remember that in New Haven once,
where the fearless and the bearded poet
chanting Om on the city green
calmed a crowd and forestalled a riot
by terrified police

   5.

and pink moonlight–
now lacy and faint–
is the only trace left
of the ominous and stunning Blue Blood eclipse
that slid below the horizon
just before dawn.

The Ideal World

It is not some café on the Mediterranean glittering in the sun, the ocean breezes of the spring, the smell of coffee;

it is not Yo-Yo Ma and Peter Serkin wordlessly letting us in on the intimate partly improvised conversation that is the sonata,

it is not the clamor and jabber of eighty thousand cranes after they have glided to a stop on the marshy lake, having swooped in silent descent from the heavens,

nor the fear-filled bravery of those who face down the instruments of tyranny until the opposing phalanxes dissipate in the clear air of morning,

nor the seemly colloquy of honest adversaries,

nor the bubble within which we cultivate kindness to our own,

but a crowded bus on the way home from a demonstration and a child no older than three in her mother's arms yelling the contagious chant, "The people demand social justice."

To My Wife

Then there was my awakening
in Ricadi to the swish and swirl
of three voices, barely
above whispering, words
not perceptible at all:
women's voices, yes, yours,
Hedi's, Gabi's,
syncopated with the notes
of eleven-month Roni
and nineteen-month Louis
poking in, above the fluid
variations in the trio of women,
the solos, the duets, the silences, the *tzlil*,
the pitch and timbre
of each voice distinct as they slide
from earnest softness to passion to laughter
to small chiding of the kids,
"shhhh…Lyla…sleeping,"
". . . so's Papa," who, I figure,
could lie here listening-in
forever, doing his job,
dutifully recording it all
for you.

Earthsea

In the first great scene of the story
the boy Ged reveals and exhausts himself
conjuring up fog and managing to dismantle it

into ghosts that harass the blood
thirsty invaders who chase
the taunting shapes he has fashioned

over a cliff to plunge to their deaths,
like the Hindenberg over eighty years ago,
the flames of the dirigible altered

into cold damp smoke. Thirty years ago
I read my daughter this book, now
a gift from her for the ninth birthday of her nephew,

her sister's son, for me to read again,
this time grandfather to grandson, as he curls
his lean body into mine as if we were exposed

to South Pole weather on some old expedition
and our huddle is our only way
of surviving the ice. So the great scene today is neither

the snowboarding the aunt and nephew
threw themselves into at the Snow Bowl in Vermont,

nor another grandchild, eight years old,
singing the Queen of the Night aria 7000 miles away,
ordering the killing of her consort in stunning melody,

but rather that rare moment in an alternate reality,

LeGuin's, early in Earthsea, when good and evil
for once are sharply distinguished
and the great balance of all
things has not yet been revealed.

Still, Small

I Kings 19:12

A little girl sits, her back and head to a wall, eyes closed, hands
    together
as if in prayer. A little girl sits against a wall a third of the way
from the right side of a photograph, the soles of her shoes pink

at the end of her legs, relaxed and fully extended in white tights
A three-and-a-half year old girl sits against a dirty white wall,
with children's drawings across its whole width

just above the level of her head had she been standing:
a faint array of verticals and sharp objects,
a square robot's head, perhaps, or steeples, missiles, skyscrapers,

or helicopters, and, above them, five puffy clouds. Roni sits
on eroded concrete against a wall in a pink on white
jumper and a green long-sleeved shirt, elbows at her sides,

hands clasped together just touching her slightly uplifted chin,
a thick black aura of hair around her peaceful face, a still
small silence in the heart of a small nation intoxicated and riven by
    walls.

The City

The plane hums southward down the Hudson
and wheels left tilting around the Battery,
with Liberty at the center of the arc it traces
turning north, up the East River toward La Guardia.
The great city below, the edges
of skyscrapers and streets
make perfectly sharp lines, perfectly
still and inanimate in the clear early morning air,
the two great absences only a pang now
in a passenger's mind as all of Manhattan
appears in miniature, a perfect model of itself
that can be taken in whole in a single glance
or held in a pair of cupped hands,
as if the entire beating metropolis
were a child's toy and we were giants.

Home

On this brief visit feeling the familiar mass
of short, gray Vermont days, I don't want to go on
a pawn of the drab dark places
filled with the wet sands of routine
that bury my imagination with the dullness
of a steak knife that won't cut butter
and a spider mind that plays solitaire on screen,
bets on football games, and checks emails
again. Which is why, yesterday, reading the *Odyssey*
to my seven-year-old grandson, when we get
to the scene in which Eurycleia, bathing a stranger,
is the first mortal to recognize him, her master,
her baby, lost for twenty years to someone else's war,
and I describe the old nurse running her fingers slowly
along the telltale scar on his thigh, feeling
and joyously knowing that flesh—though I've read
the scene out loud dozens of times—this time
my eyes water, and Louis starts crying, too,
and asks, "Why are we crying, Opapa?" "Oh,"
I say, "It's so happy and so sad to be home again.
Twenty years is a long time to be away." "Yes, it is,"
he agrees, nodding soberly. Yes it is.

Notes

Epigraph. William Carlos Williams, "Asphodel, That Greeny Flower." From *Pictures from Breughel.* New York: New Directions, 1962.

"Jewcap." Tomas Transtromer, "Solitude." From *The Half-Finished Heaven: Selected Poems.* Translated by Robert Bly. Minneapolis: Gray Wolf, 2017. Ralph Ellison, *Invisible Man.* New York: Random House, 1952.

"Wind Hair." William Carlos Williams, "The Descent." From *Paterson.* New York: New Directions, 1949.

"At the Movies." Aeschylus, *The Agamemnon.* From *The Complete Greek Tragedies: Volume I, Aeschylus.* Chicago: University of Chicago Press, 1953. Trans. Richmond Lattimore

"Black Panther." Rosanna Warren, "Ghost in a Red Hat." From *Ghost in a Red Hat.* New York: W.W. Norton & Company, 2011.

"Basketball." Kevin "KG" Garnett, Glen "Big Baby" Davis, and Rajon Rando played for the champion Boston Celtics basketball team in 2007–08.

"Any Misery in the Sound of the Wind." Wallace Stevens, "The Snow Man." From *Collected Poems of Wallace Stevens.* New York: Alfred A. Knopf, 1954.

"The Snorkelers." Walt Whitman, "Song of Myself." From *Leaves of Grass.* 1881.

In "Sycamores," "Lilac blossoms of courage." Robert Duncan, "A Poem Beginning with a Line by Pindar." From *The Opening of the Field.* New York: New Directions Books, 1960.

"The Silence." Yehudi Amichai, "The Diameter of the Bomb." Translated by Bernard Horn.

"Death, Rothko Said." Mark Rothko, "Address to Pratt Institute." November, 1958.

"Hope, Heartbreak." William Wordsworth, "Lines Composed a Few Miles above Tintern Abbey." 1798.

"Earthsea." Ursula K. Le Guin, *Earthsea.* New York: 1968–2001.

Acknowledgments

Thanks to Alan Feldman, my first reader, the Framingham Public Library Poetry Workshop, where many of these poems were born, and my terrific editor at Circling Rivers, Jean Huets.

Facts, Fakes, Fictions: Raynes Poetry Prize Finalists. Blue Thread Press. "My Father Speaks."

Climbing Lightly through Forests. Aqueduct Press. "Earthsea."

Devouring the Green: Fear of a Human Planet: An Anthology of New Writing. Jaded Ibis Press. "Jewcap," "Any Misery in the Sound of the Wind."

Dime Show Review. "Cinderella."

Home(less)ness: Geographies of Identity: a zine. "Raccoon."

Ibbetson Street. "Home."

Mad River Review. "Above Leuk," "To My Wife."

The Mississippi Review. "The Porch."

The New York Times. "The City."

Pomme Journal: Put into Words, My Love. "Mind, Feel."

Literary Matters. "Try to Remember."

Tupelo Quarterly. "My Father, the Swimmer."